Preface: Navigating the Pages

I0427325

Welcome to "Futures Trading Unveiled: Mastering Trends and Technologies for Profitable Strategies." This book is meticulously organized to provide you with a comprehensive journey through the intricate world of futures trading. To ensure an efficient and enriching reading experience, we have crafted a detailed index that serves as your roadmap through the diverse topics covered in each chapter.

In this section, we present the Table of Contents, offering a glimpse into the expansive knowledge awaiting you. Whether you are a seasoned trader seeking advanced strategies or a newcomer eager to understand the fundamentals, this index will guide you seamlessly through the chapters, allowing you to tailor your exploration based on your specific interests and learning objectives.

Take a moment to peruse the index, acquaint yourself with the chapters, and embark on a learning journey that delves into everything from the basics of futures contracts to the nuanced realm of psychological aspects in trading. Each chapter is designed to build upon the previous, providing a well-rounded and practical understanding of futures trading.

Dive in, explore, and let the index be your trusted companion as you navigate the pages of "Futures Trading Unveiled." Happy reading and successful trading!

Table of Contents

- **Case Studies**
  - Real-life examples of successful futures trading
  - Lessons learned from trading experiences
- **Psychological Aspects of Trading**
  - Managing emotions and discipline
  - Dealing with losses and avoiding overtrading
- **Regulatory Environment**
  - Understanding regulations governing futures trading
  - Compliance and ethical considerations
- **Advanced Strategies**
  - Options trading within futures markets
  - Spreads, arbitrage, and other advanced techniques
- **Future Trends in Futures Trading**
  - Emerging technologies and their impact
  - Evolving market trends and opportunities
- **Conclusion**
  - Summarizing key concepts
  - Encouraging continuous learning and adaptation

Introduction

Futures markets represent a dynamic and integral component of the global financial landscape, playing a pivotal role in shaping economic activities and providing a platform for participants to manage risk, speculate, and discover prices for a wide array of assets. This introduction delves into the essence of futures markets, offering insights into their significance within the broader financial framework.

Overview of Futures Markets

Futures markets serve as organized platforms where participants engage in contracts to buy or sell assets at predetermined prices and dates in the future. These contracts, known as futures contracts, are standardized, facilitating a level playing field for market participants. Commodities, financial instruments, and indices are among the myriad assets traded within these markets. The standardized nature of futures contracts fosters liquidity, price discovery, and risk management.

One distinctive feature of futures markets is the ability to trade both long (buy) and short (sell) positions. This flexibility allows market participants to capitalize on price movements in either direction, creating opportunities for profit irrespective of market trends. The futures market's efficiency in reflecting current and future market conditions contributes to its appeal for a diverse range of participants, including institutional investors, speculators, and corporations seeking to hedge against price fluctuations.

Importance of Futures Trading in Financial Markets

The significance of futures trading extends far beyond the trading floors and electronic platforms where contracts change hands. These markets play a crucial role in the broader financial ecosystem, influencing various stakeholders and contributing to overall market stability.

- **Price Discovery**: Futures markets are at the forefront of price discovery, providing real-time information about market expectations and sentiments. The prices established in futures contracts serve as benchmarks for the underlying assets, influencing pricing mechanisms across financial markets.

- **Risk Management**: One of the primary functions of futures trading is risk management. Participants, known as hedgers, use futures contracts to mitigate the impact of adverse price movements in the underlying assets. This risk mitigation mechanism is vital for businesses, farmers, and investors, allowing them to plan and operate with a level of certainty in an inherently uncertain environment.

- **Liquidity and Efficiency**: Futures markets enhance overall market liquidity by providing a venue for buying and selling standardized contracts. This liquidity not only facilitates seamless trade execution but also contributes to market efficiency by narrowing bid-ask spreads and reducing the impact of large trades on prices.

- **Portfolio Diversification**: Investors utilize futures markets to diversify their portfolios and gain exposure to different asset classes. This diversification strategy helps manage overall risk by spreading investments across a range of instruments with potentially uncorrelated price movements.

In conclusion, the dynamic nature and multifaceted roles of futures markets make them a cornerstone of the global financial system. From serving as a barometer for market sentiments to providing essential risk management tools, futures trading influences a myriad of financial decisions, making it imperative for market participants and observers to comprehend its nuances and intricacies. This exploration into the overview and importance of futures trading sets the stage for a deeper dive into the mechanics, strategies, and evolving landscape of these vital financial markets.

Understanding Futures Contracts

Futures contracts are the lifeblood of futures markets, providing a standardized framework for participants to engage in buying and selling agreements for various assets. This chapter delves into the definition, types, and key components that shape the dynamics of futures contracts.

Definition of Futures Contracts

At its core, a futures contract is a legal agreement between two parties to buy or sell a specific quantity of an asset at a predetermined price on a future date. These contracts are standardized to ensure uniformity across the market, facilitating efficient trading and risk management. Futures contracts can be based on a variety of underlying assets, including commodities, financial instruments, indices, and more.

Types of Futures Contracts

1. **Commodity Futures Contracts**: Tied to the price of physical commodities such as gold, oil, or agricultural products. These contracts are instrumental for producers and consumers in managing price fluctuations.

2. **Financial Futures Contracts**: Linked to financial instruments like currencies, interest rates, or stock indices. Investors often use these contracts for speculative purposes or to hedge against financial market risks.

3. **Index Futures Contracts**: Derive their value from a stock market index, providing a convenient way for investors to gain exposure to broader market movements without holding individual stocks.

4. **Currency Futures Contracts**: Allow participants to speculate on the future exchange rates between different currencies, serving as a risk management tool for businesses exposed to currency fluctuations.

Key Components of Futures Contracts

Understanding the key components of futures contracts is crucial for participants to navigate these markets effectively.

1. **Expiration Date**: Every futures contract has a specified expiration date, indicating when the contract will cease to exist. It's the date by which the contract must be settled, either by physical delivery of the underlying asset or through a cash settlement.

2. **Contract Size**: Also known as the contract multiplier, this represents the quantity of the underlying asset covered by a single futures contract. It varies depending on the type of asset and is standardized to facilitate trading.

3. **Tick Size**: Refers to the minimum price movement allowed for a futures contract. The tick size is crucial for price quoting and determines the smallest increment by which the contract's price can change.

By comprehending the nuances of futures contracts, participants can make informed decisions, whether they are seeking to manage risk, speculate on price movements, or diversify their investment portfolios. The next chapters will further explore the intricacies of trading strategies, risk management, and the broader ecosystem of futures markets.

Market Fundamentals

Understanding market fundamentals is essential for any participant in futures trading. This chapter explores two crucial aspects: the supply and demand dynamics that drive price movements and the profound impact of economic indicators on futures prices.

Supply and Demand Dynamics

1. **Supply and Demand Basics**: At the heart of market fundamentals lies the interaction between supply and demand. When demand for a commodity or financial instrument exceeds its supply, prices tend to rise, and vice versa. Futures markets provide a platform for participants to express their views on these dynamics.

2. **Price Discovery**: Futures markets play a crucial role in price discovery by aggregating information from various participants. The constant flow of buy and sell orders helps establish fair market prices, reflecting the collective expectations of supply and demand forces.

3. **Speculation and Hedging**: Speculators aim to profit from anticipated price movements, while hedgers use futures contracts to protect against adverse price changes. The interplay between these groups contributes to the ebb and flow of supply and demand within the market.

4. **Market Liquidity**: Understanding supply and demand dynamics is integral to gauging market liquidity. Liquid markets, characterized by ample buying and selling interest, generally provide smoother trade execution and more accurate price discovery.

Impact of Economic Indicators on Futures Prices

1. **Economic Indicators Defined**: Economic indicators are statistical metrics used to evaluate economic conditions. Key indicators include GDP growth, unemployment rates, inflation, and consumer confidence. These factors influence investor sentiment and, consequently, futures prices.

2. **Leading, Lagging, and Coincident Indicators**: Investors categorize economic indicators based on their timing relative to economic cycles. Leading indicators offer insights into future trends, lagging indicators confirm trends, and coincident indicators move in tandem with the overall economy.

3. **Interest Rates and Central Bank Policies**: Changes in interest rates, driven by central bank policies, can significantly impact futures prices. Investors closely monitor interest rate announcements, as they influence the cost of capital and can affect the attractiveness of different assets.

4. **Global Events and Geopolitics**: Events such as geopolitical tensions, natural disasters, and global economic shifts can trigger volatility in futures markets. Traders need to stay attuned to these external factors as they can swiftly alter supply and demand dynamics.

By mastering the intricacies of supply and demand and staying informed about economic indicators, futures traders can gain a competitive edge. The next chapters will delve into risk management strategies, technical and fundamental analysis, and practical approaches to navigating the dynamic landscape of futures trading.

Risk Management

Effective risk management is the bedrock of successful futures trading. This chapter delves into the paramount importance of risk assessment and introduces various tools and strategies essential for navigating the uncertainties inherent in the futures markets.

Importance of Risk Assessment in Futures Trading

1. **Preserving Capital**: Risk assessment in futures trading is synonymous with preserving capital. By identifying and quantifying potential risks, traders can safeguard their investment capital, ensuring they have the resources to participate in future opportunities.

2. **Mitigating Losses**: Futures markets can be volatile, and adverse price movements are inevitable. Risk assessment enables traders to anticipate and mitigate potential losses, preventing catastrophic impacts on their portfolios.

3. **Psychological Stability**: Knowing the risks involved instills psychological stability. Traders who understand and manage risks are less prone to emotional decision-making, maintaining discipline and resilience even in challenging market conditions.

4. **Long-Term Viability**: Successful futures trading is a marathon, not a sprint. A systematic approach to risk management ensures the longevity of a trading career, allowing participants to weather the ups and downs of the market over time.

Tools and Strategies for Managing Risk

1. **Stop-Loss Orders**: Implementing stop-loss orders helps limit potential losses by automatically triggering a sell order when an asset's price reaches a predetermined level. This tool is crucial for disciplined risk management.

2. **Diversification**: Spreading investments across various asset classes can mitigate risk by reducing exposure to the fluctuations of any single market. Diversification is a fundamental strategy to achieve a balanced and resilient portfolio.

3. **Position Sizing**: Determining the appropriate size for each position based on risk tolerance and account size is vital. Position sizing ensures that no single trade excessively influences the overall portfolio.

4. **Risk-Reward Ratio**: Evaluating the potential risk and reward of a trade before entering is a key aspect of risk management. Maintaining a favorable risk-reward ratio ensures that potential profits outweigh potential losses.

5. **Use of Derivatives for Hedging**: Futures contracts can be employed for hedging purposes, helping market participants offset risks associated with price fluctuations in the underlying assets. This is particularly relevant for businesses dealing with commodities.

6. **Volatility Analysis**: Understanding market volatility is essential for risk management. Volatility indicators can guide traders in adjusting position sizes and stop-loss levels to align with the prevailing market conditions.

By integrating these tools and strategies into their trading plans, participants can navigate the complexities of futures markets with a calculated and resilient approach.

The subsequent chapters will further explore technical and fundamental analysis, trading strategies, and the psychological aspects of futures trading

Technical Analysis

Technical analysis is a fundamental aspect of futures trading, providing traders with tools to interpret price charts and make informed decisions. This chapter delves into two key elements of technical analysis: chart patterns and trend analysis, along with popular indicators used to predict price movements.

Chart Patterns and Trend Analysis

1. Support and Resistance Levels:

   - Support Levels: Price levels where an asset often stops falling and might bounce back.

   - Resistance Levels: Price levels where an asset often faces selling pressure.

2. Trendlines:

   - Uptrend: Connects higher lows, indicating a bullish trend.

   - Downtrend: Connects lower highs, signaling a bearish trend.

   - Sideways Trend: Indicates a range-bound market with no clear upward or downward movement.

3. Chart Patterns:

   - Head and Shoulders: Reversal pattern signaling a potential trend change.

   - Double Tops and Bottoms: Indicate potential reversal points in the market.

   - Triangles (Symmetrical, Ascending, Descending): Represent periods of consolidation before price continuation or reversal.

4. Candlestick Patterns:

  - Doji: Indicates market indecision.

  - Engulfing Patterns: Signal potential trend reversals.

  - Hammer and Hanging Man: Highlight potential trend changes.

Indicators for Predicting Price Movements

1. Moving Averages:

  - Simple Moving Average (SMA) and Exponential Moving Average (EMA): Smooth out price data to identify trends.

  - Golden Cross and Death Cross: Signal potential bullish or bearish trends based on the crossover of moving averages.

2. Relative Strength Index (RSI):

  - Measures the speed and change of price movements, helping identify overbought or oversold conditions.

3. MACD (Moving Average Convergence Divergence):

  - Consists of MACD line, signal line, and histogram, providing insights into the strength and direction of a trend.

4. Bollinger Bands:

  - Consist of a middle band (SMA) and upper/lower bands representing volatility. Useful for identifying potential reversal or continuation points.

5. Fibonacci Retracements:

- Utilizes Fibonacci ratios to identify potential support or resistance levels based on historical price movements.

6. Volume Analysis:

   - Examining trading volumes alongside price movements can confirm the strength of a trend or signal potential reversals.

7. Stochastic Oscillator:

   - Measures the location of a current price in relation to its price range over a defined period, helping identify overbought or oversold conditions.

By incorporating these technical analysis tools, traders can gain insights into market trends, potential reversal points, and optimal entry or exit positions. It's important to note that technical analysis is just one facet of trading, and combining it with fundamental analysis and risk management strategies can enhance overall decision-making. The subsequent chapters will explore fundamental analysis, trading strategies, and the psychological aspects of futures trading.

Fundamental Analysis

Fundamental analysis is a critical approach to understanding the intrinsic value of assets and making informed trading decisions based on economic factors. This chapter delves into the process of analyzing economic factors affecting futures markets and harnessing news and events to shape decision-making.

Analyzing Economic Factors Affecting Futures Markets

1.**Economic Indicators**:

-*GDP (Gross Domestic Product)*: Measures a country's economic output.

-*Unemployment Rate*: Indicates the health of the job market and overall economic stability.

-*Inflation Rate*: Reflects the rate at which general prices for goods and services rise.

2.**Interest Rates**:

- Central banks' decisions on interest rates can impact the attractiveness of various assets, influencing futures prices.

3.**Government Policies**:

- Changes in fiscal and monetary policies can have profound effects on the economy and subsequently on futures markets.

4.**Supply and Demand for Commodities**:

- Understanding the fundamentals of the specific commodities being traded is crucial. Factors such as weather conditions, geopolitical events, and technological advancements can impact supply and demand.

5.Global Events:

- Geopolitical events, natural disasters, and global economic shifts can create volatility in futures markets. Keeping an eye on global developments is essential for anticipating market movements.

Using News and Events to Make Informed Decisions

1.**Market Sentiment**:

  - News and events shape market sentiment. Positive news can drive bullish sentiment, while negative news may lead to a bearish outlook.

2.**Earnings Reports**:

  - For stocks and equity indices, corporate earnings reports can significantly impact prices. Positive earnings may lead to upward movements, while disappointing results can cause declines.

3.**Central Bank Announcements**:

  - Statements and decisions from central banks, particularly regarding interest rates and monetary policy, can influence currency and bond futures.

4.**Government Reports**:

  - Economic reports released by government agencies, such as employment data, trade balances, and manufacturing indices, provide valuable insights into economic health.

5.**Natural Disasters and Political Events**:

  - Unforeseen events, such as natural disasters or political turmoil, can have immediate and profound effects on futures markets. Traders need to stay vigilant for sudden shifts in market dynamics.

By incorporating fundamental analysis and staying abreast of relevant news and events, traders can gain a deeper understanding of the forces shaping market movements. Combining this approach with technical analysis and effective risk management strategies contributes to a well-rounded decision-making process in the dynamic world of futures trading. The subsequent chapters will further explore advanced strategies, trading psychology, and emerging trends in futures trading.

Trading Strategies

In the vast landscape of futures trading, various strategies cater to different risk appetites and time horizons. This chapter explores the distinctions between day trading and swing trading, along with the strategies of scalping, trend following, and contrarian approaches.

Day Trading vs. Swing Trading

1.**Day Trading**:

-*Time Horizon*: Involves opening and closing positions within the same trading day.

-*Frequency*: Executes multiple trades in a single day to capitalize on intraday price movements.

-*Risk Tolerance*: Requires close monitoring and quick decision-making. Intraday volatility can be higher, demanding a higher risk tolerance.

2.**Swing Trading**:

-*Time Horizon*: Positions are held for a period ranging from a few days to several weeks.

-*Frequency*: Fewer trades compared to day trading, allowing traders to capture price swings over a more extended timeframe.

-*Risk Tolerance*: Generally, a lower level of intraday stress compared to day trading. Requires patience to wait for swing opportunities to unfold.

Scalping, Trend Following, and Contrarian Strategies

1.**Scalping**:

-*Objective*: Capitalizes on small price changes, aiming for quick, small profits.

-*Execution*: Involves numerous trades throughout the day, each targeting minimal price movements.

-*Risk Management*: Requires tight stop-loss orders due to the small profit margins.

2.**Trend Following**:

-*Objective*: Identifies and follows prevailing market trends.

-*Execution*: Enters trades in the direction of the established trend, aiming to ride the trend until signs of reversal.

-*Risk Management*: Emphasizes letting profits run and cutting losses short, adhering to the trend's momentum.

3.**Contrarian Strategies**:

-*Objective*: Takes positions against prevailing market sentiment.

-*Execution*: Enters trades when market sentiment is excessively bullish or bearish, expecting a reversal.

- *Risk Management*: Requires careful consideration of potential market turns and the ability to withstand short-term market sentiment against the trade.

Choosing a trading strategy depends on various factors, including risk tolerance, time commitment, and market conditions. Traders often combine elements from different strategies or adapt their approach based on changing market dynamics. As the journey in futures trading unfolds, the ability to select and implement suitable strategies becomes a key determinant of success. The subsequent chapters will delve into advanced strategies, the psychological aspects of trading, and the evolving landscape of futures markets

Brokerage and Platforms

Selecting a trustworthy futures broker and utilizing efficient trading platforms are critical decisions for futures traders. This chapter guides traders through the process of choosing a reliable broker and explores essential features of trading platforms and tools.

Choosing a Reliable Futures Broker

1. **Regulation and Compliance**:

   - Ensure the broker is regulated by relevant authorities, providing a layer of oversight and protection for traders.

2. **Reputation and Track Record**:

   - Research the broker's reputation in the industry and review client testimonials. A long and positive track record is often indicative of reliability.

3. **Transaction Costs**:

   - Consider commission fees, spreads, and any additional charges. Transparent and competitive pricing structures are essential for cost-effective trading.

4. **Range of Markets**:

   - Evaluate the variety of futures markets and instruments offered by the broker. A diverse range allows traders to explore different sectors.

5. **Technology and Platforms**:

   - Assess the trading platforms provided by the broker. Look for user-friendly interfaces, advanced charting tools, and reliable execution speed.

6. **Customer Support**:

   - Reliable customer support is crucial. Check for availability, responsiveness, and the ability to resolve issues promptly.

7. **Educational Resources**:

   - Brokers offering educational materials and resources can be valuable for traders, especially those new to futures markets.

8. **Risk Management Features**:

   - Ensure the broker provides risk management tools such as stop-loss orders, limit orders, and margin requirements to help traders protect their capital.

Exploring Trading Platforms and Tools

1. User-Friendly Interface:

   - A well-designed, intuitive platform streamlines the trading process, making it easier for traders to execute orders and analyze markets.

2. Charting and Analysis Tools:

   - Advanced charting tools with technical indicators, drawing tools, and customization options are essential for in-depth analysis.

3. Execution Speed and Reliability:

   - A robust and reliable trading platform is crucial for executing orders swiftly, especially in fast-paced futures markets.

4. Market Data:

   - Access to real-time market data is vital. Evaluate the depth of market data provided by the platform, including price quotes and order book information.

5. Mobile Accessibility:

   - A mobile trading app enables traders to monitor and execute trades on the go. Ensure the mobile platform offers essential features without compromising functionality.

6. Risk Management Features:

   - The platform should support various risk management tools, such as setting stop-loss and take-profit orders, to enhance trading discipline.

7. Back-Testing and Simulation:

   - Some platforms offer back-testing and simulation features, allowing traders to test strategies in historical market conditions before implementing them in live trading.

By carefully considering these factors when selecting a futures broker and exploring trading platforms, traders can set themselves up for a smoother and more effective trading experience. As technology continues to evolve, staying informed about the latest advancements in trading platforms becomes essential for remaining competitive in the dynamic futures markets. Subsequent chapters will delve into advanced strategies, risk management, and the psychological aspects of futures trading.

Developing a Trading Plan

A well-structured trading plan is a cornerstone for success in futures trading. This chapter outlines the crucial steps in developing a trading plan, focusing on setting goals and objectives and establishing a disciplined trading routine.

Setting Goals and Objectives

1. Define Your Purpose:

 - Clarify why you are engaging in futures trading. Whether it's capital growth, income generation, or portfolio diversification, a clear purpose guides your strategy.

2. Set Realistic Financial Goals:

 - Establish achievable and measurable financial objectives. This might include profit targets, risk tolerance levels, and expectations for returns.

3. Time Horizon:

 - Determine your time horizon for trading. Are you a short-term day trader or a longer-term swing trader? Align your goals with your preferred trading style.

4. Risk-Reward Ratio:

- Define your acceptable risk-reward ratio for trades. This ensures that potential losses are mitigated and profits are optimized in line with your risk tolerance.

5. Evaluate and Adapt:

- Regularly assess and adjust your goals as market conditions, personal circumstances, and trading experience evolve.

Creating a Disciplined Trading Routine

1. Set Clear Trading Hours:

- Establish specific hours for trading that align with your strategy and lifestyle. This helps maintain focus during market hours and prevents overtrading.

2. Pre-market Preparation:

- Conduct thorough analysis before the market opens. Review economic indicators, news, and overnight developments to inform your trading decisions.

3. Risk Management Protocols:

- Define clear risk management rules, including maximum loss thresholds per trade and overall account risk. Adhering to these limits safeguards your capital.

4. Trade Entry and Exit Criteria:

- Clearly outline your criteria for entering and exiting trades. This includes technical signals, fundamental factors, and any other indicators that inform your decision-making process.

5. Journaling and Review:

- Maintain a trading journal to record each trade, along with your thought process and emotions. Regularly review your journal to identify patterns, strengths, and areas for improvement.

6. Continuous Learning:

   - Allocate time for ongoing education and skill development. Staying informed about market trends, new strategies, and emerging technologies enhances your trading capabilities.

7. Emotional Discipline:

   - Develop strategies to manage emotions during trading. This includes recognizing and mitigating stress, anxiety, and impulsiveness that can arise in the dynamic environment of futures trading.

8. Regular Assessments:

   - Periodically review your trading routine and make adjustments based on performance, changes in the market, or personal circumstances. Adaptability is key to long-term success.

By adhering to a well-defined trading plan, traders can navigate the complexities of futures markets with greater confidence and discipline. Regularly revisiting and refining your plan ensures its relevance and effectiveness over time. The subsequent chapters will explore advanced strategies, the psychological aspects of trading, and emerging trends in the dynamic world of futures trading

Case Studies

Examining real-life examples of successful futures trading provides valuable insights and lessons for traders. This chapter presents a couple of illustrative case studies, highlighting key strategies and lessons learned from these experiences.

Case Study 1: Trend Following in Commodities

Background:

A trader identified a strong upward trend in the price of a specific commodity, driven by increasing demand and supply constraints. Recognizing the potential for sustained price appreciation, the trader employed a trend-following strategy.

Strategy:

1. Entered a long position as the commodity's price broke out of a consolidation phase, confirming the upward trend.

2. Implemented a systematic approach to risk management, setting a trailing stop-loss to protect against adverse price movements.

3. Allowed profits to run by trailing the stop-loss along with the rising trend, aiming to capture maximum gains during the upward movement.

Outcome:

The trade resulted in significant profits as the commodity continued its upward trajectory. The disciplined adherence to the trend-following strategy, coupled with effective risk management, contributed to the success of the trade.

Lessons Learned:

1. Patience Pays Off: Successful trend following often requires patience to ride out short-term fluctuations in pursuit of more significant long-term gains.

2. Adaptability: While the initial analysis identified a strong trend, the trader remained adaptable, adjusting the stop-loss as the trend evolved.

Case Study 2: Hedging Against Price Volatility

Background:

A business involved in the production of a key commodity faced uncertainty due to volatile market conditions. Concerned about potential price fluctuations impacting profitability, the business decided to use futures contracts to hedge against adverse price movements.

Strategy:

1. Analyzed historical price trends and market dynamics to determine the optimal timing for implementing hedges.

2. Entered into futures contracts to sell a portion of the anticipated commodity production at predetermined prices, providing price certainty.

3. Monitored the market regularly and adjusted hedge positions as needed based on changing market conditions.

Outcome:

The hedging strategy protected the business from losses caused by adverse price movements. Even though the market experienced volatility, the predetermined prices secured through futures contracts allowed the business to maintain profitability.

Lessons Learned:

1. Risk Mitigation: Hedging is a powerful tool for managing price risk, providing businesses with a level of certainty in uncertain market conditions.

2. Regular Review: Periodic reassessment of market conditions is crucial for adjusting hedge positions and ensuring alignment with the business's risk management goals.

These case studies underscore the importance of strategic planning, disciplined execution, and adaptability in futures trading. Learning from real-life examples helps traders refine their approaches and navigate the dynamic and often unpredictable nature of the futures markets.

Psychological Aspects of Trading

The psychological aspects of trading play a crucial role in a trader's success. This chapter explores strategies for managing emotions and maintaining discipline, along with addressing losses and avoiding the pitfalls of overtrading.

Managing Emotions and Discipline

1. Emotional Awareness:

   - Acknowledge and understand the emotions that arise during trading, such as fear, greed, and excitement. Awareness is the first step in managing these emotions effectively.

2. Establishing a Trading Plan:

   - Having a well-defined trading plan provides a structured framework, reducing emotional decision-making. Stick to your plan, and avoid making impulsive decisions based on emotional reactions.

3. Risk Management:

   - Implementing sound risk management practices helps mitigate the emotional impact of losses. Knowing that each trade has predefined risk and potential rewards can ease anxiety.

4. Taking Breaks:

- Trading can be intense, and continuous monitoring of markets can lead to emotional fatigue. Take regular breaks to refresh your mind and maintain focus.

5. Visualization Techniques:

- Visualizing successful trades and positive outcomes can help build confidence and reduce anxiety. It's a technique used by many successful traders to reinforce a positive mindset.

Dealing with Losses and Avoiding Overtrading

1. Accepting Losses as Part of the Process:

- Losses are an inevitable part of trading. Accepting them as a natural occurrence and learning opportunity can prevent emotional distress.

2. Analyzing Losses Objectively:

- Instead of dwelling on losses emotionally, analyze them objectively. Identify what went wrong, learn from the experience, and use it to refine your trading strategy.

3. Avoiding Revenge Trading:

- A significant loss may trigger a desire to recoup losses quickly. This emotional response, known as revenge trading, often leads to impulsive decisions and increased risk. Avoid it by sticking to your plan.

4. Setting Daily and Weekly Limits:

   - Establishing limits on the number of trades or total losses in a day or week helps prevent overtrading and ensures you don't compound losses.

5. Monitoring Trading Psychology Metrics:

   - Some trading platforms offer metrics related to trading psychology, such as stress levels and risk tolerance. Monitoring these metrics can provide insights into emotional well-being during trading.

6. Journaling:

   - Keep a trading journal to record not only your trades but also your emotional state during each trade. Reflecting on past entries can help you identify patterns in emotional responses.

Remember, trading is as much about managing your psychology as it is about analyzing markets. Developing a disciplined mindset, staying emotionally resilient, and learning from both successes and setbacks contribute significantly to long-term success in futures trading. The subsequent chapters will delve into advanced strategies, market trends, and emerging technologies in the evolving landscape of futures trading.

Regulatory Environment

Understanding the regulatory environment is crucial for participants in futures trading. This chapter provides insights into the regulations governing futures trading and emphasizes compliance and ethical considerations.

Regulations Governing Futures Trading

1. Commodity Futures Trading Commission (CFTC):

   - In the United States, the CFTC is the primary regulatory body overseeing futures and options markets. It ensures fair and transparent markets while protecting market participants from fraud and manipulation.

2. Securities and Exchange Commission (SEC):

   - While the CFTC oversees most futures and commodities markets, the SEC regulates specific financial futures contracts and options. This includes certain equity index futures.

3. National Futures Association (NFA):

   - The NFA is a self-regulatory organization that works in conjunction with the CFTC. It sets standards and rules for its member firms and individuals engaged in futures trading.

4. Financial Conduct Authority (FCA):

   - In the United Kingdom, the FCA regulates financial markets, including futures trading. It aims to ensure market integrity and protect consumers.

5. European Securities and Markets Authority (ESMA):

   - ESMA oversees financial markets in the European Union, including regulating futures and derivatives markets. It focuses on harmonizing regulations across EU member states.

6. International Regulatory Cooperation:

   - Various international bodies work towards fostering cooperation among regulatory authorities globally. This includes the International Organization of Securities Commissions (IOSCO) and the Financial Stability Board (FSB).

Compliance and Ethical Considerations

1. Know Your Customer (KYC):

   - Traders and brokers must adhere to KYC procedures, verifying the identity of their clients. This helps prevent fraud and ensures compliance with anti-money laundering (AML) regulations.

2. Market Integrity:

   - Upholding market integrity is paramount. Engaging in manipulative practices, spreading false information, or engaging in any form of market abuse is strictly prohibited.

3. Risk Disclosure:

   - Traders and brokers must provide clear and comprehensive risk disclosures to clients. This ensures that participants are aware of the potential risks associated with futures trading.

4. Conflicts of Interest:

 - Firms and individuals involved in futures trading must manage and disclose any conflicts of interest. This ensures fair and unbiased treatment of clients.

5. Data Protection and Privacy:

 - Compliance with data protection laws is crucial. Traders and brokers must ensure the secure handling of client information, respecting privacy and confidentiality.

6. Continuous Education and Training:

 - Staying informed about regulatory updates and industry best practices is a key ethical consideration. Continuous education and training help market participants remain compliant and uphold ethical standards.

Adherence to regulations and ethical considerations not only ensures legal compliance but also contributes to the overall stability and reputation of the futures markets. Traders and market participants should stay informed about regulatory changes and foster a culture of ethical conduct within the industry. The subsequent chapters will explore advanced strategies, technological trends, and emerging dynamics in futures trading.

Advanced Strategies

In the dynamic world of futures trading, participants often employ advanced strategies to gain a competitive edge. This chapter explores options trading within futures markets and introduces advanced techniques such as spreads, arbitrage, and other sophisticated approaches.

Options Trading within Futures Markets

1. Covered Call Strategy:

   - Involves holding a long position in a futures contract while simultaneously writing (selling) a call option on the same asset. This strategy generates income from option premiums while limiting potential upside gains.

2. Protective Put Strategy:

   - Combines a long futures position with the purchase of a put option to hedge against potential downside risk. This strategy provides insurance against adverse price movements.

3. Straddle and Strangle Strategies:

- Straddle involves buying both a call and a put option with the same strike price and expiration date, anticipating significant price volatility. Strangle is similar but involves different strike prices. Traders using these strategies profit from substantial price movements, regardless of direction.

4. Butterfly Spread:

- Combines options with three strike prices to create a low-risk, low-reward strategy. It involves buying one lower strike option, selling two middle strike options, and buying one higher strike option.

Spreads, Arbitrage, and Other Advanced Techniques

1. Calendar Spreads:

- Involves simultaneously buying and selling futures contracts with different expiration dates. Traders aim to profit from price differences influenced by time decay and market expectations.

2. Inter-Commodity Spreads:

- Traders exploit price differentials between related but distinct commodities. For example, a trader may simultaneously buy soybean futures and sell corn futures if historical price relationships suggest a potential convergence.

3. Statistical Arbitrage:

- Utilizes quantitative models and statistical analysis to identify mispricings between related financial instruments. Traders execute trades based on historical patterns and statistical probabilities.

4. Pairs Trading:

- Involves taking long and short positions in two correlated assets to profit from relative price movements. Traders aim to capitalize on the convergence or divergence of the two asset prices.

5. Delta-Neutral Trading:

  - Balances the delta of options positions to make the overall position insensitive to small price movements. This strategy minimizes directional risk and focuses on volatility and time decay.

6. High-Frequency Trading (HFT):

  - Utilizes algorithms and computerized systems to execute a large number of orders at extremely high speeds. HFT strategies exploit short-term market inefficiencies and price discrepancies.

These advanced strategies require a deep understanding of market dynamics, sophisticated risk management techniques, and often involve complex calculations. Traders employing these strategies should have a robust understanding of the associated risks and be prepared to adapt to rapidly changing market conditions. As technology continues to advance, incorporating quantitative analysis and algorithmic trading approaches becomes increasingly common in the pursuit of alpha in futures markets. The subsequent chapters will explore technological trends, emerging dynamics, and risk management strategies in the evolving landscape of futures trading.

Covered Call Strategy

The covered call strategy is a popular options trading strategy employed by investors seeking to generate income from existing stock holdings while potentially limiting upside gains. This strategy involves holding a long position in an underlying asset, typically stocks, and simultaneously selling call options against that position.

Key Components of the Covered Call Strategy:

1. Long Stock Position:

 - The investor holds a certain number of shares of the underlying stock in their portfolio. This position serves as the "covered" part of the strategy.

2. Call Option Sale:

 - Simultaneously with the stock purchase, the investor sells call options. Each call option represents the right (but not the obligation) for the option buyer to purchase the underlying stock at a specified price (strike price) within a set time frame (until expiration).

3. Income Generation:

 - The investor receives a premium for selling the call options. This premium provides immediate income, which can enhance overall returns, especially in markets with lower volatility.

How the Covered Call Strategy Works:

1. Income Generation:

   - By selling call options, the investor collects premiums, which can partially offset potential losses or enhance gains from the stock position.

2. Limited Upside Potential:

   - The sale of call options imposes an obligation to sell the stock at the agreed-upon strike price if the option is exercised. This caps the potential profit from the stock's upward price movement.

3. Downside Protection:

   - The income generated from selling call options provides some downside protection. The premium received lowers the breakeven point for the overall position, reducing potential losses.

4. Expiration and Outcome:

   - If the stock price remains below the strike price at expiration, the call options expire worthless, and the investor keeps the premium. If the stock price rises above the strike price, the investor may be obligated to sell the stock at the agreed-upon price.

Considerations for Implementing a Covered Call Strategy:

1. Strike Price Selection:

   - Choosing an appropriate strike price is crucial. It should be a level at which the investor is willing to sell the stock, considering both potential gains and the desired exit point.

2. Expiration Date:

   - Investors must decide on the expiration date of the call options. Shorter expirations offer more frequent premium income but limit flexibility, while longer expirations provide greater flexibility but reduce premium income frequency.

3. Market Outlook:

   - This strategy is most effective in neutral to slightly bullish markets. In strongly bullish markets, the capped upside potential may be a limiting factor.

4. Risk Management:

   - Investors should have a clear understanding of the risks involved. Monitoring the stock's performance, staying informed about market conditions, and having exit strategies in place are crucial elements of risk management.

The covered call strategy is a conservative approach suitable for income-oriented investors with a moderately bullish outlook on the underlying stock. While it provides income and some downside protection, investors must carefully assess the trade-offs between potential gains and limitations on upside profits. As with any investment strategy, thorough research, risk management, and ongoing monitoring are essential components of success.

While the covered call strategy is commonly associated with stocks, it can be adapted for use in futures trading, albeit with some key differences. In a futures context, the covered call strategy involves holding a long position in a futures contract on an underlying asset and simultaneously selling call options on that futures contract.

Adapting the Covered Call Strategy to Futures:

1. Long Futures Position:

   - Instead of owning the physical stock, the investor holds a long position in a futures contract on a specific underlying asset. This could be a commodity, financial instrument, or equity index.

2. Call Option Sale on Futures:

   - Simultaneously with the futures purchase, the investor sells call options on that specific futures contract. Each call option provides the buyer with the right (but not the obligation) to assume the long futures position.

3. Income Generation:

   - Similar to the stock-covered call strategy, the investor receives premiums from selling call options. This premium income can enhance overall returns.

Key Considerations for Covered Call Strategy in Futures:

1. Underlying Asset Selection:

   - Futures contracts cover a broad range of underlying assets, including commodities (e.g., gold, oil), financial instruments (e.g., interest rate futures), and equity indices. Investors should choose an underlying asset based on their market outlook and objectives.

2. Strike Price and Expiration:

 - Selecting an appropriate strike price and expiration date is crucial. The strike price should reflect the level at which the investor is comfortable potentially selling the futures contract. The expiration date determines the timeframe for the covered call strategy.

3. Market Conditions:

 - As with the stock-covered call strategy, the effectiveness of the strategy in futures trading depends on market conditions. It is most suitable in neutral to slightly bullish markets.

4. Rolling Positions:

 - Futures contracts have expiration dates, and as they approach expiration, investors may need to roll their positions by closing out the existing contract and opening a new one with a later expiration date. This requires careful management and may impact the premium income.

5. Leverage and Margin:

 - Futures contracts are leveraged instruments, and investors need to be aware of the associated margin requirements. The use of leverage amplifies both potential gains and losses.

Advantages and Risks:

1. Income Generation:

 - Similar to the stock-covered call strategy, one of the primary advantages is the generation of income through premium collection.

2. Limited Upside Potential:

 - The covered call strategy in futures also imposes a cap on potential profits, as the investor may be obligated to sell the futures contract at the agreed-upon price if the call option is exercised.

3. Risk of Assignment:

  - There is a risk that the call option may be exercised, leading to the obligation to sell the futures contract. This risk is present until the expiration date, and investors need to be prepared for potential assignment.

4. Market Movement:

  - If the market experiences significant adverse movements, the strategy may not provide adequate downside protection, especially if the futures contract position faces substantial losses.

The covered call strategy in futures can be a valuable tool for income-oriented investors looking to enhance returns and manage risk. However, as with any trading strategy, thorough understanding, ongoing monitoring, and effective risk management are essential for success. Investors should also be aware of the specific nuances and risks associated with futures contracts and options on futures.

Lets consider a real-life example of a covered call strategy with futures:

1. Asset and Contract Selection:

   - Assume an investor is bullish on the price of crude oil.

   - The investor buys one crude oil futures contract (e.g., WTI crude oil futures).

2. Execution of Covered Call:

   - Simultaneously, the investor sells a call option on the same crude oil futures contract to generate premium income.

   - Let's say the investor sells a call option with a strike price of $70 per barrel.

3. Scenario Analysis:

   - Scenario 1 (Bullish):

     - If the price of crude oil rises, the investor benefits from the appreciation of the futures contract.

     - The call option may be exercised by the buyer, resulting in the investor selling the futures contract at the agreed-upon strike price of $70 per barrel. The investor still profits from the price increase up to the strike price.

   - Scenario 2 (Neutral or Slightly Bearish):

     - If the price of crude oil remains relatively stable or slightly decreases, the investor keeps the premium received from selling the call option.

     - The call option may expire worthless, and the investor retains both the premium and the long futures position.

   - Scenario 3 (Significant Bearish Movement):

- If the price of crude oil drops significantly, the premium income from the call option helps offset the losses on the futures position.

- However, the investor still faces downside risk, and the strategy may not fully protect against substantial declines.

4. Potential Outcomes:

- The covered call strategy provides a balance between potential upside gains and downside protection through the premium income.

- It's crucial for the investor to monitor market conditions and manage the position accordingly, such as rolling the call option if needed or closing the position before expiration.

Remember, while covered calls can provide income and limited protection, they also have risks. Investors should carefully assess their risk tolerance and market outlook before implementing such strategies.

Arbitrage Strategy in Futures

Arbitrage is a trading strategy that involves exploiting price discrepancies of the same asset across different markets or exchanges. In the context of futures trading, various arbitrage opportunities may arise due to temporary mispricings between related contracts. One common type of arbitrage in futures markets is the "cash and carry" or "arbitrage via futures" strategy.

Cash and Carry Arbitrage:

1. Understanding the Concept:

   - Cash and carry arbitrage takes advantage of pricing differences between the spot (cash) market and the futures market for the same underlying asset. The strategy involves buying the underlying asset in the spot market, simultaneously selling a futures contract, and then holding the position until the futures contract expires.

2. Components of the Strategy:

   - Buy Spot (Cash): The trader purchases the actual asset in the spot market.

   - Sell Futures: Simultaneously, the trader sells a futures contract for the same asset, which is typically priced higher due to factors like interest rates and carrying costs.

3. Holding Period:

   - The trader holds the position until the expiration of the futures contract. The goal is to profit from the convergence of spot and futures prices at expiration.

4. Profit Mechanism:

- If executed correctly, the trader profits from the difference between the initial lower spot price and the higher futures price, minus transaction costs and carrying costs.

Key Considerations for Cash and Carry Arbitrage:

1. Carrying Costs:

   - Traders must account for the costs associated with holding the physical asset until the expiration of the futures contract. These costs may include storage, insurance, and financing.

2. Interest Rates:

   - The interest rate environment plays a crucial role in cash and carry arbitrage. Higher interest rates may increase the cost of financing the spot position, impacting potential profits.

3. Dividends (for Equities):

   - For equity futures, traders need to consider dividends. If the underlying asset pays dividends, the cash and carry arbitrage strategy must factor in the impact of dividend payments.

4. Execution Timing:

   - Timely execution is essential in arbitrage strategies. Price discrepancies may be short-lived, and efficient execution is crucial to capturing the potential profit.

5. Transaction Costs:

   - Traders should carefully assess transaction costs, including brokerage fees and any other expenses associated with executing and maintaining the arbitrage position.

Example:

Let's consider an example with a commodity like oil. If the spot price of oil is $50 per barrel, and the one-month futures contract is priced at $52, a trader could buy oil in the spot market for $50, sell a one-month futures contract at $52, and hold the position until expiration. If, at expiration, the spot and futures prices converge at $51, the trader would profit from the $1 price difference.

Risks and Challenges:

1. Market Conditions:

   - Market conditions may change, affecting the profitability of the arbitrage strategy. Unexpected events, such as supply disruptions or changes in market sentiment, can impact price relationships.

2. Execution Risks:

   - Delays or difficulties in executing trades may erode potential profits. Efficient execution is crucial in arbitrage strategies.

3. Liquidity:

   - Low liquidity in either the spot or futures market can pose challenges. Thinly traded markets may result in wider bid-ask spreads and increased execution risk.

4. Regulatory Risks:

   - Regulatory changes or interventions can influence market dynamics and impact the effectiveness of arbitrage strategies.

While cash and carry arbitrage is a well-known strategy, traders need to carefully assess market conditions, costs, and execution factors to successfully capitalize on pricing discrepancies. It requires a combination of market expertise, efficient execution capabilities, and a deep understanding of the specific dynamics of the asset being traded.

Protective Put Strategy in Futures: Real Case Explanation

The protective put strategy, often known as a "married put," involves holding a long position in an underlying asset while simultaneously purchasing a put option on that asset to protect against potential downside risk. Let's explore a real-case scenario applying the protective put strategy in the context of crude oil futures.

Background:

Consider a scenario where an investor holds a long position in crude oil futures due to expectations of rising oil prices. However, the investor is concerned about potential downside risks, such as geopolitical tensions impacting oil supply or unexpected shifts in global demand.

Trade Setup:

1. Existing Long Position:

   - The investor has a long position in crude oil futures, reflecting a bullish outlook on oil prices.

2. Purchase of Put Option:

   - To protect against potential downside risk, the investor decides to implement a protective put strategy. They purchase a put option with a strike price that aligns with their risk tolerance and the level at which they are willing to limit potential losses.

   - Example: The current price of crude oil futures is $70 per barrel. The investor purchases a put option with a strike price of $65, providing the right to sell crude oil futures at $65.

3. Expiration and Cost Considerations:

   - The investor selects an expiration date for the put option, taking into account the time frame over which they want protection. They also factor in the cost of purchasing the put option, considering it as an insurance premium to safeguard their long position.

Outcome Scenarios:

1. Scenario 1 - Rising Prices:

   - If crude oil prices rise as anticipated, the investor benefits from the profit on the long futures position. The put option expires worthless, and the investor incurs the cost of the option premium as a form of insurance.

2. Scenario 2 - Downside Protection:

   - If unforeseen events lead to a decline in crude oil prices, the protective put strategy comes into play. The investor can exercise the put option, selling crude oil futures at the predetermined strike price, thereby limiting losses.

   - Example: If crude oil prices fall to $60 per barrel, the investor exercises the put option, selling futures at the higher strike price of $65. This provides a level of downside protection.

Considerations and Risks:

1. Cost of Protection:

   - The cost of purchasing the put option is an upfront expense. This cost needs to be weighed against the potential benefits of protecting against downside risk.

2. Expiration and Rolling:

   - Traders should be mindful of the expiration date of the put option. If the protective put strategy is part of a longer-term position, investors may need to roll the put option to maintain continuous protection.

3. Monitoring and Adjustments:

   - Market conditions change, and investors should regularly assess the need for continued downside protection. Adjustments to the strike price or expiration date may be necessary based on evolving circumstances.

4. Opportunity Cost:

   - If the market remains bullish and the protective put is not utilized, the investor incurs the cost of the put option as an opportunity cost. This cost is justified by the insurance against potential downside risks.

 Conclusion:

In this real-case scenario, the investor strategically employs a protective put strategy in crude oil futures to balance their bullish outlook with a proactive risk management approach. The protective put acts as a form of insurance, providing a predetermined level of downside protection while allowing the investor to participate in potential upside gains. As with any trading strategy, careful consideration of costs, ongoing monitoring, and adjustments based on market conditions are integral to its success.

Straddle and Strangle Strategies in Futures: Real Case Explanation

The straddle and strangle strategies are volatility-based options trading strategies that involve simultaneously buying a call and a put option. These strategies are employed when traders anticipate significant price movements but are uncertain about the direction. Let's explore a real-case scenario applying the straddle and strangle strategies in the context of equity index futures.

Background:

Consider a scenario where an investor expects a major market-moving event, such as an earnings announcement or an economic data release, but is uncertain about whether the impact will result in a substantial upward or downward movement in the S&P 500 index.

Trade Setup:

1. Straddle Strategy:

   - The investor decides to implement a straddle strategy by simultaneously buying a call option and a put option with the same strike price and expiration date on S&P 500 index futures.

   - Example: The S&P 500 index is currently at 4,000. The investor purchases both a call and a put option with a strike price of 4,000 and an expiration date aligned with the anticipated market-moving event.

2. Strangle Strategy:

   - Alternatively, the investor may choose to implement a strangle strategy. This involves buying a call option with a higher strike price and a put option with a lower strike price, both with the same expiration date.

   - Example: The investor buys a call option with a strike price of 4,050 and a put option with a strike price of 3,950, aligning with the same expiration date.

Outcome Scenarios:

1. Scenario 1 - Significant Price Movement:

- If the anticipated market-moving event results in a substantial price movement in either direction, the investor profits from the profitable leg of the straddle or strangle.

- Example: If the S&P 500 index experiences a sharp increase to 4,100, the call option in the straddle or strangle strategy becomes profitable.

2. Scenario 2 - Limited Movement:

- If the market response is muted, and the S&P 500 index stays close to the initial level of 4,000, both the call and put options may experience losses due to time decay.

- Example: If the S&P 500 index hovers around 4,000, both the call and put options may expire worthless, resulting in a loss equal to the initial premium paid for the options.

Considerations and Risks:

1. Cost of Options:

- The cost of purchasing both a call and a put option can be a significant upfront expense. Traders need to carefully assess whether the expected price movement justifies this cost.

2. Time Decay:

- Options are subject to time decay, meaning their value decreases as time passes. If the market doesn't move significantly, the trader may face losses due to time decay.

3. Volatility Impact:

- The profitability of straddle and strangle strategies is heavily influenced by the magnitude of the price movement. Higher volatility generally benefits these strategies.

Conclusion:

In this real-case scenario, the investor strategically employs straddle and strangle strategies in S&P 500 index futures to capitalize on anticipated market volatility surrounding a significant event. The success of these strategies depends on the extent of the market movement, making them valuable tools for traders expecting volatility but uncertain about the direction. Traders should carefully assess the risk-reward dynamics and be prepared for potential losses if the expected price movement doesn't materialize

Butterfly Spread in Futures: Real Case Explanation

The butterfly spread is an options trading strategy that involves using three strike prices to create a position with limited risk and limited profit potential. This strategy profits from minimal price movement in the underlying asset. Let's explore a real-case scenario applying the butterfly spread strategy in the context of crude oil futures.

Background:

Imagine a scenario where an options trader believes that crude oil prices are likely to remain stable in the short term, with minimal price fluctuations. The trader wants to capitalize on this expectation using a butterfly spread.

Trade Setup:

1. Analysis:

   - The trader analyzes historical volatility and market conditions and concludes that crude oil prices are likely to experience minimal movement in the near term.

2. Butterfly Spread Construction:

   - The trader decides to implement a butterfly spread by using call options on crude oil futures. They choose three strike prices: A (lower strike), B (middle strike), and C (higher strike).

   - Example:

     - Buy 1 call option with a strike price of $70 (A)

     - Sell 2 call options with a strike price of $75 (B)

     - Buy 1 call option with a strike price of $80 (C)

3. Position Size:

   - The trader adjusts the position size to reflect their risk tolerance and market outlook. The net effect of the strategy is a net debit position, as the trader pays a premium for the options.

Outcome Scenarios:

1. Scenario 1 - Minimal Price Movement:

   - If crude oil prices remain stable within the range of strike prices B (middle strike), the trader profits from the time decay of the options sold at strike B.

   - Example: If the price of crude oil at expiration is $75, the options at strike B expire worthless, and the trader profits from the premium received.

2. Scenario 2 - Outside the Range:

   - If crude oil prices move significantly beyond the range of strikes B, the butterfly spread may result in a loss. The risk is limited to the initial premium paid for the options.

   - Example: If the price of crude oil at expiration is $80 or higher, the options at strike B may result in losses, but the risk is limited.

Considerations and Risks:

1. Limited Profit Potential:

   - The butterfly spread has limited profit potential. The maximum profit occurs if the underlying asset closes at the middle strike price at expiration.

2. Risk-Reward Ratio:

   - Traders should carefully assess the risk-reward ratio to ensure that the potential profit justifies the initial premium paid for the butterfly spread.

3. Volatility Impact:

   - The strategy benefits from low volatility. High volatility may result in wider price movements, impacting the profitability of the butterfly spread.

Conclusion:

In this real-case scenario, the trader strategically employs a butterfly spread strategy in crude oil futures to take advantage of an expected period of minimal price movement. The structured use of call options at three different strike prices allows the trader to benefit from time decay while limiting both potential profits and losses. As with any options strategy, careful consideration of market conditions, risk management, and adjustments based on evolving circumstances are crucial for success. The butterfly spread serves as a tool for traders seeking to capitalize on a narrow range of price movement in the underlying asset.

Calendar Spread in Futures: Real Case Explanation

A calendar spread, also known as a time spread or horizontal spread, involves simultaneously buying and selling futures contracts with the same underlying asset but different expiration dates.

Let's explore a real-case scenario applying the calendar spread strategy in the context of wheat futures.

Background:

Consider a scenario where a commodities trader anticipates seasonal factors affecting wheat prices. The trader expects increased volatility leading up to the harvest season but believes prices will stabilize afterward. To capitalize on this expectation, they decide to implement a wheat calendar spread.

Trade Setup:

1. Analysis:

   - The trader analyzes historical price patterns for wheat futures and identifies a seasonal trend where prices tend to increase leading up to the harvest and stabilize afterward.

2. Calendar Spread Construction:

   - The trader executes a calendar spread by simultaneously:

     - Buying one wheat futures contract expiring in the current month (near-month contract).

     - Selling one wheat futures contract expiring in a later month (far-month contract).

   - Example:

     - Buy one near-month wheat futures contract with expiration in June.

     - Sell one far-month wheat futures contract with expiration in September.

3. Position Size:

   - The trader determines the position size based on risk tolerance and market expectations. The goal is to benefit from potential price movements during the near-term while mitigating risk through the offsetting far-month contract.

Outcome Scenarios:

1. Scenario 1 - Seasonal Increase and Stabilization:

   - If wheat prices follow the anticipated seasonal pattern, increasing leading up to the harvest and stabilizing afterward, the trader profits from the near-month contract while the far-month contract may incur losses. The overall outcome depends on the magnitude of the price movement.

   - Example: If wheat prices rise in June due to increased demand before the harvest and then stabilize in September, the trader benefits from the price increase in the near-month contract and accepts a limited loss in the far-month contract.

2. Scenario 2 - Unanticipated Market Events:

   - If unforeseen events impact wheat prices differently than expected, the trader may experience losses on one leg of the spread while potentially offsetting gains on the other leg.

   - Example: Unexpected weather conditions lead to a decline in wheat prices in June. The trader may incur losses on the near-month contract but could potentially offset some of those losses with gains on the far-month contract if it is less affected.

Considerations and Risks:

1. Market Conditions:

   - Understanding the seasonal patterns and factors influencing the commodity is crucial. Unanticipated events can impact the effectiveness of the calendar spread.

2. Rolling Positions:

   - As the near-month contract approaches expiration, the trader may need to roll the position by closing the expiring contract and opening a new one in a later month to maintain the spread.

3. Costs and Margins:

   - Traders should be aware of transaction costs, including commissions and fees, associated with executing and maintaining the calendar spread. Additionally, margin requirements need to be considered.

Conclusion:

In this real-case scenario, the trader strategically employs a calendar spread strategy in wheat futures, capitalizing on expected seasonal patterns in wheat prices. The structured use of near-month and far-month contracts allows the trader to benefit from anticipated price movements while managing risk. As with any futures trading strategy, thorough analysis, risk management, and adaptability to changing market conditions are integral for success. The calendar spread serves as a tool for traders seeking to navigate seasonal trends and capitalize on expected price movements in futures markets.

Inter-Commodity Spreads in Futures: Real Case Explanation

Inter-commodity spreads involve trading the price difference between related but distinct commodities. These spreads can be used to capitalize on pricing divergences driven by various factors. Let's explore a real-case scenario applying an inter-commodity spread strategy in the context of precious metals – gold and silver futures.

Background:

Consider a scenario where a commodities trader observes a historical price relationship between gold and silver and anticipates a temporary divergence due to changing market dynamics. The trader believes that silver prices will outperform gold in the short term.

Trade Setup:

1. Analysis:

   - The trader analyzes historical price relationships, market trends, and fundamental factors affecting both gold and silver futures.

2. Inter-Commodity Spread Construction:

   - The trader decides to implement an inter-commodity spread by:

     - Selling gold futures contracts.

     - Simultaneously buying an equivalent value of silver futures contracts.

   - Example:

     - Sell one gold futures contract.

     - Buy an equivalent value of silver futures contracts.

3. Position Size:

- The trader determines the position size based on risk tolerance, account size, and market expectations. The goal is to capitalize on the expected divergence in prices.

Outcome Scenarios:

1. Scenario 1 - Expected Divergence:

  - If silver prices outperform gold, as anticipated, the trader profits from the trade. The profit is realized when the trader closes the spread by buying back gold futures at a lower price and selling silver futures at a higher price.

  - Example: If silver prices rise while gold prices remain stable or decline, the trader benefits from the price difference when closing the spread.

2. Scenario 2 - Unexpected Events:

  - If unforeseen events impact the precious metals market differently than expected, the trader may face losses on the spread.

  - Example: Unexpected economic data affecting industrial demand for silver or geopolitical events impacting safe-haven demand for gold could lead to unexpected price movements.

Considerations and Risks:

1. Correlation Analysis:

  - Traders should analyze the historical correlation between the two commodities involved in the spread. Understanding their typical price relationship provides insights into potential spread movements.

2. Fundamental Factors:

  - Consideration of supply and demand fundamentals, geopolitical events, and macroeconomic trends influencing each commodity is crucial for making informed spread trading decisions.

3. Risk Management:

  - Setting stop-loss orders, monitoring market conditions, and having a clear exit strategy are essential components of risk management when trading inter-commodity spreads.

4. Market Liquidity:

  - Traders should be mindful of liquidity in both commodities involved in the spread. Thinly traded markets may impact the execution of spread trades.

Conclusion:

In this real-case scenario, the trader strategically employs an inter-commodity spread strategy in gold and silver futures to capitalize on anticipated short-term price divergences. The structured use of simultaneous buy and sell positions in related commodities allows the trader to benefit from relative price movements. As with any trading strategy, thorough analysis, risk management, and adaptability to changing market conditions are integral for success. Inter-commodity spreads offer traders opportunities to diversify their strategies and capitalize on relative price movements between related assets.

Statistical Arbitrage in Futures: Real Case Explanation

Statistical arbitrage involves exploiting statistical patterns or relationships between financial instruments to make profitable trades. Let's explore a real-case scenario applying statistical arbitrage in the context of equity index futures, specifically the S&P 500 and NASDAQ 100.

Background:

Consider a scenario where a quantitative trader identifies a historical correlation between the S&P 500 and NASDAQ 100 indices. The trader observes that when the correlation deviates from its historical average, there's a statistical tendency for the indices to converge.

Trade Setup:

1. Quantitative Analysis:

  - The trader uses statistical techniques to analyze the historical price movements of the S&P 500 and NASDAQ 100 indices. They calculate the correlation coefficient and identify periods where the correlation diverged significantly from its historical average.

2. Pair Selection:

  - Based on the analysis, the trader selects the S&P 500 and NASDAQ 100 futures contracts as a suitable pair for statistical arbitrage due to their historical correlation.

3. Trade Execution:

  - The trader executes a statistical arbitrage strategy by:

    - Going long on the underperforming index (if the correlation suggests it should catch up).

    - Going short on the outperforming index (if the correlation suggests it should regress).

- Example:

 - If the NASDAQ 100 has outperformed the S&P 500 beyond what the historical correlation would suggest, the trader goes long on S&P 500 futures and short on NASDAQ 100 futures.

4. Position Sizing and Risk Management:

 - The trader determines the position sizes based on statistical models and risk management parameters. The goal is to capitalize on the expected convergence while managing potential risks.

Outcome Scenarios:

1. Scenario 1 - Convergence:

 - If the historical correlation reverts to its average, causing the indices to converge, the trader profits from the convergence. The profit is realized when the trader closes the positions.

 - Example: If the NASDAQ 100 experiences a correction or underperforms relative to the S&P 500, the statistical arbitrage strategy profits from the expected convergence.

2. Scenario 2 - Deviation Continues:

 - If unexpected events or factors lead to a continued deviation in the correlation, the trader may face losses. Effective risk management is crucial in limiting potential downsides.

 - Example: If unforeseen market dynamics cause the NASDAQ 100 to maintain its outperformance, the statistical arbitrage strategy may result in losses.

Considerations and Risks:

1. Data Quality and Analysis:

- Accurate historical data and robust statistical analysis are essential for identifying meaningful patterns and relationships between financial instruments.

2. Model Calibration:

   - Statistical models used for position sizing and risk management need to be carefully calibrated to current market conditions.

3. Monitoring and Adaptability:

   - Markets evolve, and statistical relationships may change. Regular monitoring and adaptability to changing market dynamics are critical for the success of statistical arbitrage strategies.

Conclusion:

In this real-case scenario, the quantitative trader strategically employs statistical arbitrage in S&P 500 and NASDAQ 100 futures based on historical correlations. The structured use of statistical analysis allows the trader to identify potential opportunities for profit when the indices converge. As with any quantitative strategy, thorough analysis, model calibration, and continuous monitoring are integral components for success in statistical arbitrage.

Pairs Trading in Futures: Real Case Explanation

Pairs trading is a strategy that involves trading two correlated assets with the expectation that the historical price relationship between them will revert to its mean. Let's explore a real-case scenario applying pairs trading in the context of crude oil futures – specifically, trading the price relationship between Brent and WTI crude oil.

Background:

Imagine a scenario where a trader observes that the prices of Brent and WTI crude oil tend to move together historically, but occasionally, they deviate from their typical relationship. The trader believes that these deviations are temporary and present opportunities for pairs trading.

Trade Setup:

1. Correlation Analysis:

   - The trader conducts a statistical analysis to determine the historical correlation between the prices of Brent and WTI crude oil futures. They identify periods when the correlation deviates significantly from its mean.

2. Pair Selection:

   - Based on the analysis, the trader selects Brent and WTI crude oil futures as a suitable pair for pairs trading due to their historical correlation.

3. Trade Execution:

   - The trader executes the pairs trading strategy by:

     - Going long on the underperforming asset (if it has deviated below its historical relationship).

     - Going short on the outperforming asset (if it has deviated above its historical relationship).

- Example:

  - If Brent crude oil has historically traded at a premium to WTI, but the current spread widens beyond its typical relationship, the trader goes long on WTI and short on Brent.

4. Position Sizing and Risk Management:

  - The trader determines the position sizes based on risk management parameters. Effective risk management is crucial to limit potential losses in case the deviation persists.

Outcome Scenarios:

1. Scenario 1 - Mean Reversion:

  - If the historical correlation between Brent and WTI reverts to its mean, causing the spread between them to narrow, the trader profits from the mean reversion. The profit is realized when the trader closes the positions.

  - Example: If geopolitical tensions cause Brent crude to temporarily trade at a higher premium than its historical average, and the spread reverts, the pairs trading strategy profits.

2. Scenario 2 - Deviation Continues:

  - If unexpected events or factors lead to a continued deviation in the correlation, the trader may face losses. Effective risk management is crucial in limiting potential downsides.

  - Example: If unforeseen changes in supply and demand dynamics result in a persistent deviation between Brent and WTI prices, the pairs trading strategy may result in losses.

Considerations and Risks:

1. Correlation Stability:

   - Pairs trading relies on the stability of the correlation between the selected assets. Changes in market dynamics or external factors can impact the effectiveness of the strategy.

2. Risk Management:

   - Careful position sizing, setting stop-loss orders, and monitoring the trade are essential components of risk management in pairs trading.

3. Market Conditions:

   - Pairs trading may be more effective in certain market conditions, such as range-bound markets, where mean-reverting behavior is more likely.

Conclusion:

In this real-case scenario, the trader strategically employs pairs trading in Brent and WTI crude oil futures based on historical correlations. The structured use of statistical analysis allows the trader to identify potential opportunities for profit when the spread between the assets deviates from its typical relationship. As with any pairs trading strategy, thorough analysis, risk management, and adaptability to changing market conditions are integral for success. Pairs trading offers traders a systematic approach to capitalize on mean-reverting behavior between correlated assets.

Delta-Neutral Trading in Futures: Real Case Explanation

Delta-neutral trading involves creating a position with offsetting deltas to ensure that the overall delta of the portfolio is close to zero. Let's explore a real-case scenario applying delta-neutral trading in the context of options on equity index futures, specifically the S&P 500.

Background:

Consider a scenario where an options trader expects moderate volatility in the S&P 500 index but is uncertain about the market direction. The trader aims to implement a delta-neutral strategy to profit from changes in implied volatility.

Trade Setup:

1. Volatility Analysis:

   - The trader analyzes historical and implied volatility of the S&P 500 index to identify periods of expected volatility.

2. Options Selection:

   - Based on the analysis, the trader selects options contracts on S&P 500 futures with different strike prices and expiration dates. The goal is to create a delta-neutral position.

3. Delta Calculations:

   - The trader calculates the deltas of the selected options positions. Delta represents the sensitivity of the option price to changes in the underlying asset's price.

4. Delta-Neutral Position:

   - The trader adjusts the position by buying or selling options contracts to offset the deltas. The objective is to maintain a portfolio delta close to zero.

- Example:

  - If the trader buys call options with positive deltas, they may offset these by selling an equivalent amount of put options with negative deltas, creating a delta-neutral position.

Outcome Scenarios:

1. Scenario 1 - Moderate Volatility:

  - If the market experiences moderate volatility within the expected range, the delta-neutral position aims to profit from changes in implied volatility. The trader realizes gains from the time decay of options.

  - Example: Implied volatility increases slightly, leading to higher option premiums. The trader profits as the value of the options in the portfolio increases.

2. Scenario 2 - Unexpected Volatility Spike:

  - If an unexpected event causes a significant spike in volatility, the delta-neutral position may experience losses. However, these losses may be mitigated by the gains from the time decay of options.

  - Example: A sudden market event leads to a spike in implied volatility. While the delta-neutral position may incur losses, the gains from time decay partially offset the impact.

Considerations and Risks:

1. Option Greeks Management:

  - Besides delta, traders need to manage other option Greeks (e.g., gamma, theta, vega) to maintain the desired risk profile in a delta-neutral position.

2. Adjustments and Rebalancing:

  - Delta-neutral positions require constant monitoring, and adjustments may be necessary to rebalance the deltas as market conditions change.

3. Market Conditions:

  - Delta-neutral strategies may perform better in certain market conditions, such as periods of expected volatility without a clear market trend.

Conclusion:

In this real-case scenario, the options trader strategically employs delta-neutral trading in S&P 500 futures options to capitalize on changes in implied volatility. The trader aims to create a position with minimal directional bias, profiting from time decay and changes in option premiums. As with any options trading strategy, careful analysis, ongoing monitoring, and adjustments based on market conditions are crucial for success in delta-neutral trading. Delta-neutral strategies offer traders a way to navigate uncertain market directions while focusing on volatility as a potential source of profit.

High-Frequency Trading (HFT) in Futures: Real Case Explanation

High-Frequency Trading (HFT) involves executing a large number of orders at extremely high speeds, taking advantage of market inefficiencies and price discrepancies. Let's explore a real-case scenario applying HFT in the context of currency futures trading.

Background:

Consider a scenario where an HFT firm specializes in currency futures trading. The firm has developed sophisticated algorithms capable of processing vast amounts of market data in real-time and executing trades at speeds measured in microseconds.

Trade Setup:

1. Algorithmic Strategy Development:

  - The HFT firm develops complex algorithms designed to exploit microsecond-level price discrepancies in currency futures markets. These algorithms leverage statistical arbitrage, market-making, and latency arbitrage strategies.

2. Co-location and Low Latency Infrastructure:

  - The firm invests in co-located servers placed in close proximity to the exchange's data center to minimize latency. Low-latency infrastructure, including high-speed data feeds and direct market access, is crucial for rapid order execution.

3. Statistical Arbitrage:

  - One algorithm focuses on statistical arbitrage by identifying short-term price divergences between related currency futures contracts. The algorithm rapidly executes buy or sell orders to capitalize on these brief pricing discrepancies.

4. Market-Making:

 - Another algorithm acts as a market-maker, placing limit orders on both the bid and ask sides. The firm aims to profit from the bid-ask spread as traders execute market orders against their quotes.

 Outcome Scenarios:

1. Scenario 1 - Profitable Statistical Arbitrage:

 - If the statistical arbitrage algorithm identifies and exploits short-term pricing discrepancies successfully, the HFT firm realizes profits from rapid, high-frequency trades.

 - Example: The algorithm detects a temporary mispricing between Euro and US Dollar futures contracts, executes rapid trades to capitalize on the discrepancy, and closes positions as the prices converge.

2. Scenario 2 - Market-Making Profits:

 - If the market-making algorithm effectively manages bid-ask spreads and captures trading volume, the HFT firm profits from the high-frequency execution of numerous small trades.

 - Example: The firm's market-making algorithm consistently provides liquidity by placing tight bid-ask spreads. Traders executing market orders contribute to the firm's profitability through the bid-ask spread.

 Considerations and Risks:

1. Technology Investment:

- HFT requires significant investments in cutting-edge technology, including hardware, software, and co-location services, to maintain a competitive edge in execution speed.

2. Risk Management:

- Managing risk in HFT involves implementing safeguards against unexpected events, market disruptions, or algorithmic errors that could lead to significant losses.

3. Market Regulations:

- HFT firms need to comply with and adapt to evolving market regulations, including measures to prevent market manipulation and ensure fair and orderly trading.

Conclusion:

In this real-case scenario, an HFT firm specializing in currency futures employs sophisticated algorithms and high-speed infrastructure to execute trades at a microsecond level. The firm's strategies, including statistical arbitrage and market-making, showcase the versatility of HFT in capturing profits from rapid market movements and providing liquidity. As with any HFT strategy, continuous adaptation to market conditions, rigorous risk management, and compliance with regulations are essential for success in the fast-paced world of high-frequency trading.

Setting profitable trades with futures here's a step-by-step guide with an example:

Step 1: Market Analysis

Example:

Consider analyzing the crude oil futures market.

Step 2: Identify Trends and Patterns

Example:

Identify a bullish trend in crude oil prices based on technical analysis, noting recent higher highs and higher lows.

Step 3: Fundamental Analysis

Example:

Check fundamental factors like global demand, geopolitical events, and supply disruptions impacting crude oil prices.

Step 4: Choose a Trading Strategy

Example:

Opt for a trend-following strategy, such as buying a crude oil futures contract.

Step 5: Set Entry Point

Example:

Wait for a pullback in crude oil prices to enter the market at a favorable price point, aligning with the overall uptrend.

Step 6: Determine Stop-Loss and Take-Profit Levels

Example:

Set a stop-loss below the recent low to manage risk. Set a take-profit level based on a reasonable price target within the uptrend.

Step 7: Calculate Position Size

Example:

Determine the position size based on the risk per trade and the distance to the stop-loss level.

Step 8: Monitor Market Conditions

Example:

Continuously monitor the crude oil market for any relevant developments that may impact the trade.

Step 9: Execute the Trade

Example:

Place the buy order for the crude oil futures contract at the chosen entry point.

Step 10: Review and Adjust

Example:

Regularly review the trade's performance and adjust the stop-loss or take-profit levels if necessary. Be prepared to exit the trade if conditions change.

Step 11: Closing the Trade

Example:

Close the trade when the price reaches the take-profit level or if there are signs of a trend reversal.

Step 12: Evaluate Results

Example:

Evaluate the profitability of the trade based on the initial analysis, identifying strengths and areas for improvement.

Important Considerations:

- *Risk Management:*

  - Set a risk-reward ratio to ensure potential profits justify potential losses.

- *Diversification:*

  - Consider diversifying your futures portfolio to spread risk across different assets.

- *Stay Informed:*

  - Keep abreast of market news and events that could impact your chosen futures market.

- *Adaptability:*

  - Be flexible and willing to adapt your strategy based on changing market conditions.

Example Summary:

In this example, a trader analyzes the crude oil futures market, identifies a bullish trend, and executes a buy order during a pullback. The trader sets clear stop-loss and take-profit levels, calculates an appropriate position size, and continuously monitors the market for adjustments.

Successful futures trading requires a disciplined approach, continuous learning, and adaptability to changing market dynamics.

Options on futures provide the holder with the right, but not the obligation, to buy (call option) or sell (put option) a futures contract at a predetermined price (strike price) on or before the expiration date. Here's a breakdown of options in futures:

Key Components:

1. Underlying Asset:

  - Options on futures derive their value from an underlying futures contract, representing an agreement to buy or sell an asset at a future date.

2. Call Option:

  - A call option gives the holder the right to buy the underlying futures contract at the agreed-upon strike price. Traders use call options to profit from potential price increases.

3. Put Option:

  - A put option gives the holder the right to sell the underlying futures contract at the agreed-upon strike price. Traders use put options to profit from potential price decreases.

4. Strike Price:

- The strike price is the price at which the option holder can buy (for a call option) or sell (for a put option) the underlying futures contract.

5. Expiration Date:

- Options on futures have a limited lifespan. The expiration date is when the option contract ceases to exist. The holder must exercise the option before or on this date.

6. Premium:

- Option buyers pay a premium to the option seller for the right to buy (call option) or sell (put option) the underlying futures contract. The premium is the upfront cost of the option.

Description of Options in Futures:

- Risk-Limited:

- Option buyers have a limited risk exposure. The maximum loss is limited to the premium paid for the option.

- Flexibility:

- Options provide flexibility to traders. Call options allow for potential profit in rising markets, while put options offer a hedge against falling markets.

- Leverage:

- Options provide leverage, enabling traders to control a larger position with a relatively small investment (the premium).

- Speculation or Hedging:

- Traders can use options for speculative purposes, aiming to profit from price movements, or for hedging to protect against adverse market movements.

- Exercise and Assignment:

- Option holders can exercise their right before or on the expiration date. If an option is in-the-money (profitable), it is likely to be exercised. Option sellers may be assigned to fulfill their obligation.

- Strategies:

- Various options strategies exist, such as covered calls, straddles, and spreads, allowing traders to customize their risk and reward profiles.

- Market Liquidity:

- Options on futures markets may have varying levels of liquidity. Highly liquid options generally have narrower bid-ask spreads.

- Settlement:

- Settlement can be either physical or cash-settled, depending on the futures contract. Physical settlement involves delivering the underlying asset, while cash settlement involves settling the profit or loss in cash.

Understanding options in futures provides traders with additional tools for risk management, speculation, and portfolio diversification. However, trading options requires a thorough understanding of the associated risks and complexities. It's advisable for individuals to educate themselves or seek advice before engaging in options trading.

Options and Futures Trading Plan: Real Case Example

Strategy: Covered Call on S&P 500 E-mini Futures

Step 1: Market Analysis

- Example:

  - Analyze the current trend and volatility in the S&P 500 E-mini futures market.

Step 2: Identify Asset and Options Contract

- Example:

  - Choose S&P 500 E-mini futures as the underlying asset and select call options with a strike price slightly above the current market price.

Step 3: Determine Trade Direction

- Example:

  - Assume a neutral to slightly bullish outlook on the S&P 500 E-mini futures.

Step 4: Set Entry Point

- Example:

  - Wait for a pullback or a period of lower volatility before entering the covered call position.

Step 5: Execute Covered Call Position

- Example:

  - Buy S&P 500 E-mini futures contracts.

  - Simultaneously sell call options against the futures contracts, selecting strike prices and expiration dates that align with the chosen strategy.

Step 6: Determine Exit Points

- Example:

  - Set a profit-taking point based on achieving the desired covered call premium.

  - Set a stop-loss point to limit potential losses if the market moves unfavorably.

Step 7: Monitor Market Conditions

- Example:

- Continuously monitor the S&P 500 E-mini futures market, assessing any developments that may impact the covered call position.

Step 8: Adjust Positions if Necessary

- Example:

- If the market moves significantly, consider adjusting the covered call position by rolling the options or adjusting the strike prices.

Step 9: Closing the Position

- Example:

- Close the covered call position when the options expire, or if the profit-taking or stop-loss points are reached.

Step 10: Review and Evaluate

- Example:

- Evaluate the performance of the covered call strategy, considering profitability, risk management effectiveness, and adaptability to market conditions.

Important Considerations:

- Risk Management:

- Ensure that the position size and risk-reward ratio align with the overall risk tolerance.

- Diversification:

  - Consider how the covered call strategy fits within the broader portfolio, aiming for diversification.

- Market News and Events:

  - Stay informed about economic indicators, earnings reports, or geopolitical events that could impact the S&P 500 E-mini futures market.

- Options Greeks Management:

  - Monitor and manage options Greeks, such as delta, gamma, and theta, to adjust the position as needed.

  Example Summary:

In this real-case example, a trader combines futures and options by executing a covered call strategy on S&P 500 E-mini futures. The plan incorporates market analysis, entry and exit points, risk management, and ongoing monitoring. The trader aims to capitalize on the neutral to slightly bullish market outlook while generating additional income through the sale of call options. Successful implementation requires diligence, adaptability, and a clear understanding of the chosen strategy's mechanics.

Future Trends in Futures Trading

1. **Emerging Technologies and Their Impact**:

a. Artificial Intelligence (AI) and Machine Learning (ML):

-Current Impact: AI and ML algorithms are currently revolutionizing trading strategies by processing vast datasets and identifying patterns.

-Future Trend: Expect an acceleration in AI's role with more sophisticated algorithms for predictive analytics, risk management, and adaptive trading strategies. This may lead to faster, more accurate decision-making in futures trading.

b. Blockchain and Smart Contracts:

-Current Impact: Blockchain technology is already enhancing transparency and security in settlement processes.

-Future Trend: Anticipate widespread adoption of blockchain for secure and transparent trade settlements. Smart contracts, powered by blockchain, could automate and streamline various aspects of futures trading, reducing counterparty risks and enhancing efficiency.

c. Quantum Computing:

-Current Impact: Quantum computing is in its early stages of exploration, particularly for complex calculations in finance.

-Future Trend: As quantum computing capabilities evolve, expect a transformative impact on risk modeling, optimization, and algorithmic complexity. Quantum computing could redefine the boundaries of computational power in futures trading.

d. High-Frequency Trading (HFT) Evolution:

-Current Impact: HFT dominates short-term trading strategies, leveraging high-speed algorithms.

-Future Trend: The evolution of HFT will involve even more sophisticated strategies, integrating AI and ML for real-time decision-making. The focus will be on nanosecond-level responsiveness to market movements.

2. **Evolving Market Trends and Opportunities:**

a. Sustainable and ESG Investing:

-Current Impact: There's a growing interest in incorporating Environmental, Social, and Governance (ESG) factors into investment decisions.

-Future Trend: Future futures trading strategies will likely integrate ESG considerations more extensively, aligning with the increasing importance of sustainability and responsible investing.

b. Decentralized Finance (DeFi):

-Current Impact: DeFi is emerging as a decentralized alternative to traditional financial services.

-Future Trend: DeFi's influence may extend into the futures trading space, giving rise to decentralized derivatives markets and challenging traditional clearing processes. Smart contracts on blockchain platforms could facilitate decentralized trading.

c. Globalization of Markets:

-Current Impact: Markets are interconnected globally through technology and shared economic events.

-Future Trend: Expect increased globalization with more cross-border trading opportunities. Futures traders will need adaptive strategies to navigate diverse economic environments and global market shifts.

d. Increased Regulatory Scrutiny:

-Current Impact: Regulatory changes are influencing trading practices, especially concerning algorithmic trading and market transparency.

-Future Trend: Regulatory scrutiny is likely to intensify. Traders will need to implement adaptive compliance measures as regulations evolve to address new technologies and trading practices.

e. Rise of Retail Trading:

-Current Impact: Retail traders, influenced by social media, are playing a more significant role in markets.

-Future Trend: The trend of increased retail involvement will likely continue, potentially influencing market dynamics. Educational resources will likely shift towards more accessible and user-friendly formats to accommodate a growing retail audience.

f. Alternative Data Utilization:

-Current Impact: Some traders leverage alternative data sources like satellite imagery and sentiment analysis for insights.

-Future Trend: Expect wider adoption of alternative data, providing traders with unique market insights. Futures traders will increasingly rely on unconventional data sources to make informed decisions.

g. Climate Risk Hedging:

-Current Impact: There is a growing awareness of climate-related risks in financial markets.

-Future Trend: Anticipate the development of futures and derivatives specifically designed for climate risk hedging. These instruments will reflect the impact of climate change on various industries, introducing new opportunities and challenges in futures trading.

h. Dynamic Risk Management:

-Current Impact: Risk management practices are generally static or periodic.

-Future Trend: The future will see the evolution of dynamic, real-time risk management systems. These systems will adapt rapidly to changing market conditions, incorporating advanced analytics for precise risk assessment and mitigation.

In navigating the future of futures trading, market participants will need to embrace these emerging technologies and adapt to evolving market trends. A proactive approach to incorporating cutting-edge tools and strategies will be crucial for success in an increasingly complex and dynamic trading environment.

Conclusion: Navigating the Future of Futures Trading

In exploring the future trends in futures trading, several key concepts emerge, pointing toward a dynamic and technologically advanced landscape. It's essential to distill these insights for a comprehensive understanding and to encourage a mindset of continuous learning and adaptation.

Summarizing Key Concepts:

1. Emerging Technologies as Catalysts:

   - Artificial Intelligence (AI), Machine Learning (ML), Blockchain, and Quantum Computing are poised to reshape futures trading by enhancing analytics, security, and computational capabilities.

2. Evolution of Trading Strategies:

- High-Frequency Trading (HFT) will evolve with more sophisticated algorithms, while decentralized finance (DeFi) and sustainable investing will influence and reshape trading strategies.

3. Globalization and Regulatory Landscape:

- Markets will become increasingly interconnected globally, demanding adaptive strategies. Regulatory scrutiny will rise, necessitating a proactive approach to compliance and risk management.

4. Retail Trading and Alternative Data:

- The rise of retail trading, influenced by social media, and the utilization of alternative data sources underscore the changing dynamics of market participation and information access.

5. Climate Risk and Dynamic Risk Management:

- Climate risk hedging will become a prominent aspect of futures trading, while dynamic risk management systems will adapt in real-time to changing market conditions.

Encouraging Continuous Learning and Adaptation:

As we stand at the intersection of technological innovation and evolving market dynamics, the success of futures traders hinges on the following principles:

1. Embrace Technological Advancements:

- Stay abreast of emerging technologies and their applications in futures trading. Embrace these tools to enhance decision-making, risk management, and operational efficiency.

2. Flexibility and Adaptability:

- Cultivate a mindset of adaptability. The ability to pivot strategies in response to changing market conditions and technological advancements is crucial for long-term success.

3. Education and Skill Development:

- Prioritize continuous learning. Stay informed about industry trends, new trading strategies, and technological developments. Invest in developing skills that align with the evolving landscape of futures trading.

4. Risk-Aware Trading:

- Maintain a vigilant approach to risk management. With the complexity of emerging technologies, understanding and mitigating risks associated with algorithmic trading, decentralized platforms, and alternative data is paramount.

5. Ethical Considerations:

- As the landscape evolves, ethical considerations in trading practices become increasingly important. Navigate the future of futures trading with a commitment to transparency, fairness, and adherence to regulatory standards.

In conclusion, the future of futures trading is an exciting frontier, filled with opportunities for those who approach it with a blend of technological acumen, adaptability, and a commitment to continuous learning. By embracing these principles, traders can navigate the evolving landscape, leveraging emerging trends to propel their success in the dynamic world of futures trading.

www.ingramcontent.com/pod-product-compliance
Lightning Source LLC
Chambersburg PA
CBHW081116290526

45795CB00006B/2142